THE ADVENTURES OF MR. D

DANIELLE TORGERSON

Archway Publishing books may be ordered through booksellers or by contacting:

Archway Publishing
1663 Liberty Drive
Bloomington, IN 47403
www.archwaypublishing.com
1 (888) 242-5904

Because of the dynamic nature of the Internet, any web addresses or links contained in this book may have changed since publication and may no longer be valid. The views expressed in this work are solely those of the author and do not necessarily reflect the views of the publisher, and the publisher hereby disclaims any responsibility for them.

Any people depicted in stock imagery provided by Thinkstock are models, and such images are being used for illustrative purposes only. Certain stock imagery © Thinkstock.

ISBN: 978-1-4808-2591-8 (sc)
ISBN: 978-1-4808-2592-5 (e)

Print information available on the last page.

Archway Publishing rev. date:2/17/2016

INTRODUCTION:

THROUGH THE FIRE

Hi, my name is Danielle Torgerson of Killeen, Tx and this is a true story of how my love for a puppy grew into a life changing story for us both.

The summer of 2007 I was working as a vet technician and it was a crazy day...I had worked for this vet for appox. 3 years and had seen some bad things...but nothing could have prepared me for this days events.

I was working with a client and her animal in one of the three exam rooms and was finishing up...when I had an unusual urge to go to another room down the hallway. This had never happened to me before and was totally against the clinic rules and policy. As I was pulled by this strange force to the room down the hall. I could hear the sobs of pain and moans of which I've never heard before. When I glanced inside the room, I saw what appeared to be a puppy on the exam table. He was in horrific pain and was also scared out of his mind. The man who owned him had brought him to the clinic claiming that the pup had been "stung" by bees, but the overwhelming stench of gasoline and burnt flesh and hair told a different story. "Someone" had poured gasoline on this baby and lit him on fire...Burning off his eyelids, melting his ears and lips, melting all of the hair off his head, down to the skull and all of the hair to his shoulders. This poor baby was here to be euthanized. I just cried and cried and could not imagine what kind of pain he was suffering through. Then my tears of pain turned to tears of anger! Who could do such a cruel act? What kind of an animal does this to another innocent life? I could not let this baby's life be extinguished before he had known the single joy that every dog should know. I wondered if he could be saved? And if he could ever have a life of normal after what he had gone through. Could he ever have a bed of his own? Go for walks down my street? Would it ever be possible that this puppy could experience love and be able to show love back? Well, "I don't know" said the Vet, "I just don't know if he's worth saving, he's in pretty bad shape and treatment if it can be carried out will be thousands of dollars".

That was all I needed to hear, besides, I had my mind made up, that puppy was going home with me. I told the man who brought the puppy in to sign over custody of the puppy to me. My boss did not want to get involved and would not call the police. I then called the office of Dr. Elaine Caplan of Austin and we went to see her for a surgical consult to see what could be done to put him back together again. It was decided that he needed major skin graft surgery to reconstruct the ears and mouth and he had hair implanted around his face, nose and head, back and shoulders and soon his condition improved, he began to function on his own.

I named him D'Artagnan (who served Louis XIV as Captain of the Musketeers of the Guard), but I called him Mr. D for short. This was just the beginning of what was to come. And in a matter of days I brought Mr. D home to meet the rest of my furball crew.

Time passed and Mr. D had grown into a large and beautiful dog and earned quite the reputation for his generous nature. "He lets the cats sleep with him and shares food with them all". But I will tell you, he has earned his stripes in protecting his momma. On the street there have been those that regard his as a beast. He is kinda scary looking at first, like a werewolf, because of all of the skin grafts, but he's just an adorable angel. And I know that because of me saving his life, that he returned the favor and helped save mine.

You see, in 2010 I was in a terrible motorcycle accident, I tried to avoid a collision with a car that came speeding through my neighborhood and came flying around the corner, it would have hit me, but I dumped the bike and hit a curb. I went airborne with the bike landing partially on top of me. Regretfully, I was not wearing a helmet and it fractured my skull. I was at the brink of death door and had to be life flighted to a hospital with a trauma center where I stayed in a coma for 12 days without any brain activity. My will stated that I was and wanted to be an organ donor, so arrangements were made that on day 13 I would be taken off of the resperator and be unplugged, so that my organs could hopefully give life to others. But while I was in that coma,

I could hear voices far away and I saw my precious Mr. D, who I knew was missing his momma. When day 13 arrived...I could hear a man who turned out to be a priest at my bedside. He was reading me my last rights and I could hear him as he prayed. Then a miracle happened, I just woke up, like I had just been asleep and my first word I said was "Mr. D". As weeks turned into month, my rehabilitation to learn to walk, speak and function dragged on. But the motivation to be back with Mr. D and my other fur babies drove me forward to show these doctors that said I would be wheelchair bound for life a thing or two. And I did show them, that not only is God great, He is our Healer and The Great Physician and still works miracles today but that our souls and ability to recover from great tragedies is in us. Now fully recovered my greatest hope is that this story will inspire people of all ages to not ever give up on yourself or your loved ones and to show people the importance of rescuing animals from shelters instead of buying animals through puppy farms. Because you will find, that the love and bond between yourself and an animal can be one that is selfless and enduring and can never be broken. I hope you can laugh and cry as we share our experiences and lives with you. And it is my prayer, that they will brighten some of your darkest days.

CHAPTER 1

PEOPLE - DUMB

"There are many wise folks with much wisdom, whom have come before us, and many whom still remain with us, but there are also fathomless amounts of those who's hopeless ignorance will remain till the end of time" - Quote by Craig Wortham, Danielles husband.

This is a true story and personal account of Mr. D and me Several weeks after Mr. D's tragic life changing and merciless torching..., a few days before his skin graft surgery, and a long way from being healed, I decided to take my precious baby boy for an outing...to get both of us out of the house and to get our minds off things a bit. I wanted to go to town to buy Mr. D a blanket to keep him warm, as all of his hair was burnt off of his head, shoulders and chest. He got cold under the ceiling fans at night while in his doggie bed on the floor. I really wanted him to sleep in my bed, but I was so afraid that I might bump him or touch his wounds and hurt him more.

So, we were heading to the local pet store...I will call it..."People Dumb" (so that the true name of the store will not be revealed, HA!) Upon arriving I carried my baby in my arms and placed him in a buggy. As we shopped through the store, we received some really strange looks and a few curious people approached and inquired about my poor boy, but low and behold...it wasn't long until I was approached by a "People Dumb" employee, that told me I would have to take my puppy and leave the store. "You are grossing out our customers with your dog" she said "And you need to leave immediately". Wow! Really!!! I couldn't believe my own ears... this is a company that is in association with ASPCA and Humane Society's across the nation and the world...and this heartless woman, that really needed her hair washed and desperately needed to see a dentist, had the nerve to ask us to leave!!! Oh No ya don't sister! When I found a manager I unloaded my 2 cents worth about what I had been asked to do by their employee, the manager hugged my neck and assured me everything was ok and that they would never, under any circumstances ask me to leave, and that the employee would be dealt with accordingly.

Well, needless to say, this did leave a very bad taste in my mouth for years about this company and we still don't darken their doors. It was so uncalled for and totally inexcusable ...It taught me a lesson...that some people don't deserve air. How could you work in a place that serves ANIMALS and not have a heart for animals, it is mind boggling.

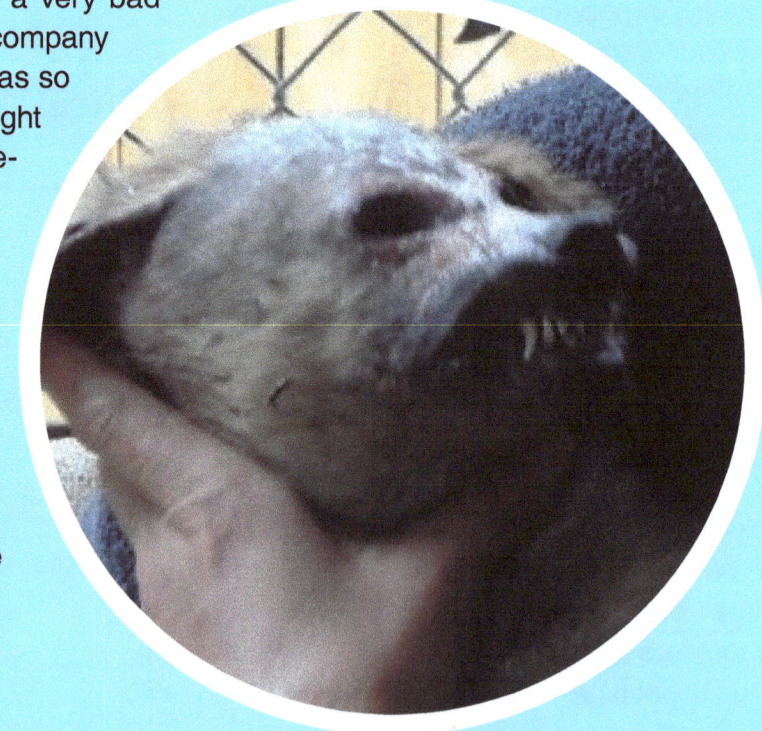

As for getting Mr. D a blanket, well, the manager told me, the one that I picked out

was on the house and he gave it to Mr. D as a present for the way we were both treated...

but still, we just decided..."People Dumb" is not, where we need to shop.

CHAPTER 2

MR. D GOES FiSHiNG

By now everyone should know my four legged Angel, Mr. D. His full name is D'Artagnan, named after the 4th Musketeer in Alexandre Dumas's classic novel "The Three Musketeers", we call him Mr. D for short or just D. He is a 8 year old lab + german shepard mix. His former owner set him on fire trying to kill him. Fate brought us together at the Vet Clinic where I worked and I adopted him, as everyone else said to put him down. From the second our eyes met, a soul connection was made that is and has been incomprehinsable by mortal terms. A love that knows no boundaries.

Just weeks after D's first grafting surgery, I decided that he and I would go for a day trip outing. Hopefully to get his mind off of the pain and for me a quiet moment.

Little did I know!!

That Saturday morning I packed a few snacks for the two of us and we headed out for a local lake, not far from our home. Even with his injuries and that stupid looking E-collar, D couldn't keep from hanging his head out the car window. He loved the wind in his face. This of course would cause quite a stir at the traffic intersections, where humans were trying to figure out what type of Animal that is with the collar, it almost caused a few wrecks...

After our arrival at the lake, I was careful to keep D close and on leash, as to not further hurt his healing wounds. But as fate would have it... the little booger pulled away and faster than greased lightning was out of my sight....

Dagnabit!!! Con Sarn it!!! You Blankety Blank!!! All of a sudden a mans voice began to scream and cuss at the top of his lungs...and the sounds of what seemed to be an elephant coming through the bush...no wait, it's Mr. D coming out of the brush, in his mouth he is carrying a large catfish and behind Mr. D is the fisherman that is chasing D and he's not a happy camper. I managed to get the fish away from D, but the Man was livid and didn't want his fish back...after giving us a bit more of his opinion...he left, trodding back through the woods in the lakes direction. I on the other hand, was admiring the great fishing abilities of my baby boy! What awesome survival skills and hey, he was bringing home the "bacon" so to speak. Oh well, I think that's why he has a Dolphin fetish...

CHAPTER 3

DOG LUNCH

A while back, before my accident, while I was still working as a vet technician, I came home for lunch. As I only had about 45 minutes I hurried home, salivating thinking about my left over steak sandwich of the chicken fried steaks I cooked the night before. Upon opening the front door I was greeted with love and lots of sniffing from all my furry children, they wanted to see how many others I had been cheating with...lol. I washed my hands and quickly put together my piece de resistance of a sandwich. But not eating quite yet, I wanted to get a little more comfortable, so I put my sandwich on the kitchen counter and pushed it against the back splash next to the coffeepot. I then ran to the bathroom real fast and as soon as I got into the bathroom I heard a very strange sound coming from the kitchen. I panicked for a moment, I could hear someone moving furniture around. It was a strange dragging sound. Silently I slid out of the bathroom door to peek around the corner into the living room, but nothing. Yet I still heard the sound of dragging furniture coming from the kitchen. I very slowly and cautiously approached the kitchen with my hairbrush in hand, ready to do business with a burglar, or fix his hair. But what I witnessed with my eyes took my breath away. My beloved boy Mr. D had evidently watched his momma use a kitchen chair before, I was watching him push a wooden table chair across the kitchen floor. He was on two legs with his two front feet on the chair and pushing it and walking it right up to the kitchen counter. There he proceeded to hop up into the chair, once in place, gingerly pulled the plate closer with his teeth, and then munched down on my Picasso of a sandwich. Not only was I astounded, but I was laughing out loud for what seemed like hours. And as I reflect on that day it reminds me of the pride I felt for my baby boy, he is so intelligent. Never, let it be said that our babies don't have the ability to think and feel. They have intelligent minds and loving souls, they also have more sense than most humans we know... And they love better, harder and without judgement. I can't wait to see what is coming next!

CHAPTER 4

MR. D AND FEATHERS

It was just another crazy monday morning from the second my feet hit the floor, I was at warp speed. Slamming and cramming coffee and toast, a quick shower, get dressed and ready for another insane work week. I always, always hug my baby boy in the morning and tell him how handsome he is and how proud of him I am and I thank him for being my Knight in Shining Armor, my protector. Of course I am speaking of Mr. D, my sweet boy that I rescued when he was 6 weeks old. Oh how I love to spoil my baby boy lol, but today was very brief and me the busy momma had to rush back to work. I yelled "bye D, see you when I come home, be a good boy" I said as I closed the door. Really??? Be a good boy huh? I'll show her how to be a good boy and what a great boy that I can be. First lets start with a little marking of some of my favorite areas and then let's move on to a major project and some fun in the bedroom, just to show her that I am currently experiencing major depression issues and "ha, ha" I can blame it on separation anxiety or better yet... blame it on the Chihuahua. "Man, that bed feels fabulous, Mr. D said, as he bounced and jumped and rolled around on the bed. "I wonder what makes it feel so good, I'm gonna make a little nest and take a little nap". "Hey wait a minute, what is that thing, a feather? Where did that come from. Oh crap, look at all the feathers, who killed all these birds? It wasn't me, I haven't even seen a bird today"!

Well, my day was a total disaster, the vet clinic where I worked was packed and overflowing out of the door with yappers and crappers lol. And when the day was finally done, all I wanted was a shower, a cold drink and my feather bed. My body was going numb, because I was so tired that I could barely turn the key at my front door. "Home, I am home, Mr. D, momma is home". Hmmm, no response! What's up with this I wondered. Extremely strange, every day, Mr. D is here to meet me at the front door without exception. But not today, my search began. From my view into the entry, I could tell he was not in the living room nor in the kitchen. But when I rounded the corner of my bedroom, it became quite clear why

I had no response. My loving boy, Mr. D, had totally shredded my goosedown German comforter! FEATHERS, FEATHERS, FEATHERS! It looked like an explosion of a truck of chickens or someone had cranked a weedeater in a cage of chickens. There on the bed with his head hanging down, feathers still clinging to his lips and more feathers raining down all over the room sat my boy Mr. D with sad eyes, he looked at me as if to say "I really didn't mean to do it and it was the other dogs that forced me into it". I hugged his neck and gave him a kiss and what did he do? He jumped off the bed and began to roll in the feathers. Yup I said, blame it on the Chihuahua lol. Gotta love 'em.

CHAPTER 5

A WARM WELCOME

After almost 2 years of engagement, we set a date and we got married. My husband Craig and I were truly soul mates, brought together by someone greater than ourselves. We like all new couples who live under one roof experienced some growing pains and this story is one that makes us chuckle.

We had at that time 5 dog babies and 4 cat babies and all of us went through growing pains. To make everyone comfortable and happy I decided to leave our bedroom door open, so our babies could have some come and go time as they needed it. I felt that since I had always left the bedroom door open it would be good for them to hear our voice and we could hear them just in case there was a moment of jealousy or disagreement. Well, I meant well...after just a few days of Craig moving into my house, I began to see changes in the babies patterns and habits. All of which was for the good. More wagging tails and lots of loving with a jealous bone thrown in here and there. My husband came in tow with one Mini Schnauzer named Sadie and one handsome cat named Booger Red (he is orange and quite the Booger). One night as we got ready for bed all the babies were settled down for the evening and Mr. D was in my bed, where he had always stayed next to me...., ever since I rescued him. Well, never dreaming what was about to happen...Craig climbed into bed and scooted over next to me. Craig was laying his head on my shoulder and we were tickling and playing with each other. This put Craig basically between myself and Mr. D, when all of a sudden WHAM! Mr. D without warning or provocation chomped down on Craigs head. Craig jumped from the bed not in pain, but more from shock that Mr. D, my baby boy, had actually bit him. Woah I thought, what's going on? But D just barked and barked and growled while jumping up and down on the bed. Craig was not mad at all, but had more hurt feelings than anything else, because he and Mr. D had become big buds. And that was all good at the ball field, or in the park, or when handing out treats, but this is different. Hey, this was his momma and NOBODY, but nobody gets next to his momma and tickles her as long as he is the ALPHA, besides it was his spot in the bed first. A little bit of alcohol and Neosporin and all was good with Craig, my big burly bear of a man. And an animal lover extrordaniar or I would not have had anything to do with him. So finally, we all settled down for a well needed nights sleep. The previous day, Craig and I had gone to town and made a few purchases. One of the items was a beautiful shirt Craig had found for himself. It was a white and tan linen shirt with wooden buttons, it was really beautiful. I had hung it on my dresser knob as a reminder to iron it the next morning. When morning came, we got up at around 7 am and got ready to feed the zoo and have our morning coffee. When our feet hit the floor, I instantly knew something was bad wrong. There hanging on my dresser knob was a shirt with big holes in it and with all the buttons gone. Bits and pieces of button and cloth were scattered through the room and down the hallway... Really??? Craig was furious, he came out of the bathroom mad as an old wet hen and stuck his feet in his slide on sandles and let out a screech that sounded as if he was mortally wounded. Now what I thought? What is it now I asked, are you ok? Now ladies and gentlemen, this could only happen here in our home, only to us, where the weird and crazy takes place. It seems as if one or more of our furry baby occupants of our home took the time and deligance not to mention perfect aim and left a little warm present for Craig in his shoe. This became quite clear it was all out war, a conspiracy to either rid themselves of change and Craig...or to give him their WARMEST WELCOME HOME to their new dad.

Today all has been forgotten and forgiven and no animals were hurt during this time,but...new shoes and a new shirt were needed, welcome home.

CHAPTER 6

MR. D AND THE TREE

By the 5th day of wet, cold, gloomy and foggy weather the sun began to shine again. Our furry babies where seriously ready for their daily dose of playing football outside. Mr. D, our largest and the Alpha of our kids was totally beside himself with mouthwatering anticipation. With tail and butt wagging, almost to the tip of his nose, his barks a pint-up boredom were released in utter joy. Holy cow Batman!! I thought my head was going to explode from all the noise of this crew lol. They looked at me as if to say "are you going to throw that ball, or do we have to jump you?" We laughed out loud at their expressed happiness.

So, I threw the ball and wow, OMG, what a catch. Mr. D went completely airborne, 3 feet in the air and caught the ball like a pro wide reciever on ESPN. Amazing, I've never seen anything like it. He caught that ball with the greatest of consistancy. The second, then the third pass. OMG, is he ever good. My forth toss was a little bit over his head, it began to bounce, but Mr. D being the focused machine that he is, no problem...but there was just one little obstacle. A couple of years back, a large freeze took out a large palm tree in our back yard. I wanted my husband to only cut down a large part of the top of the tree and leave a piece of the trunk about three foot tall. I would decorate it or use it for a planter or for the base of a birdbath, so we left it. It is approximately 24 inches around. Over the years of being exposed to the elements, it has become soft and the roots have almost let go. Well, as of today it's very loose. Thanks to Mr. D, who in the process of trying to catch the bouncing ball, traveling at the speed of a small freight train, hit it head on and never hit his breaks!! Holy Crap, I exclaimed, is he ok? He never even flinched, and he got that ball all while still wagging his tail. Wow, wow, wow, I would still be unconsious. All for the love of the game. And btw. He likes his footballs to be inflated at regulation standards, they squeak better.

CHAPTER 7

WHERE'S THE LOVE

Well, here goes another adventure in the daily life at our house, excuse me, our zoo! And again, it was our biggest 4 legged kiddo, Mr. D, that was the guilty party. It seems that everyday with this bunch of nutty animals, could be a story. So here goes...

It had been a regular hectic day around here, with the usual morning hub-bub and errands to run...but, we didn't get our usual morning play time in, as it had rained a bit during the early morning and it was to wet to play. So, when that happens we have bored and depressed little faces. As the day progressed, the sun did pop out and dried the yard enough that we felt we would give it a try. Wow!! You would have thought it was Christmas time. All the running through the house and barking and wagging to the point of knocking you off of your feet as they madly dashed for the door and out into the yard. After about 20 minutes of a lathering football practice (throwing Mr. D's football) and D not missing a single throw, we called out "Break", which is our signal for all done and game over. With his football in his mouth, Mr. D turned and ran back inside. Normally he would have brought his ball to me before going in, but not today, oh no! We came inside and I saw Mr. D in the hallway laying down, ball still in his mouth and I approached. He quickly skirted around me and shot past us running to his room. By the time I got to Mr. D's room, yes, he has his own bedroom complete with his own futon, D was looking out of the huge picture window, his ball still in his mouth, and he would not turn around to face me. I had to laugh at his stubborn determination to hang on to that ball. All of a sudden, I had a great idea, it was time to water the grass and we have an automatic sprinkler system that Mr. D loves to bark at when it is on. I knew that when I turned it on, he would have to choose to bark or to hang on to the ball. Sprinklers on, I ran to the doorway of the dogs room, Mr. D was trying to bark with the ball in his mouth, but it wasn't working out so well for him.

So, I approached him and said "give me that ball"! I kid you not, he looked me dead in my eyes and slung his head and threw that football behind the futon and against the wall which was the furtherest point and most difficult spot that he could have possibly thrown it. And then he had the audacity to actually smile about it. As if to say "I've been waiting all day for my ball, now, if you want it, you take your couchpotatoe self and dig it out on your own. Wow, did I feel the love, OMG, just another wild and crazy day at our zoo.

CHAPTER 8

GEORGE

After my life changing motorcycle accident I had to spend about 60 days in a REHAB center to learn to walk and talk and function again. It was a very sad and miserable time in my life, as I was a way from having contact with Mr. D and my babies. One morning the doctors approached me and told me that I was going home, but that they would assign home nurses to care for me for the next couple of weeks to make sure that my home recovery went well. But the very next morning after I got home from the REHAB center I began to mentally whittle down my lengthy lists of overdue chores. My PENT-UP energy and wild urge to get back to my old self was kicking in. But much to my shagrin, I was no longer the same. My balance was crazy off, all due to my massive TBI "Traumatic Brain Injury". I would trip and stumble and fall. I would walk into walls as my brain surgery had left me with major mobilization and balance issues. Not deterred, I went outside to tackle the overgrown yard. Once outside, I fired up the lawnmower and began to mow just for therapy. My adult caregivers were freaking out that I could or even would try to attempt something like this.

Well, I've never been one to shirk any kind of physical labor and besides I enjoyed mowing and I was tired of the "oh poor me" the "oh poor me pitty party", with no one but myself in attendance. After the yard was done I decided I would try to tackle a project in my washroom. I would try my hand at tiling the washroom floor. The continuous and relentless scolding from my caregivers was getting old. I was tired of them telling me what I couldn't do and not enough of them helping me do what

I could. So...I FIRED them. I then continued on with my mission to tile the washroom floor. Maybe I should have listened to them and saved it for a later year. Because the finished product looked like a couple of three year old children with ADD had played in the mud and attempted to put together a puzzle meant for adults.

IT WEREN'T a purdy sight lol! Several days passed and all of my fur babies were extremely happy that momma was home. It seemed to me like a lifetime since they had seen my face and I hadn't seen them. As a matter of fact the day that I came home Mr. D did not even recognize me until I opened my mouth to speak and he couldn't believe his momma was home. As the days passed, I got stronger and wanted to attempt more projects as I hate to set idle and not be productive. One day after breakfast I decided to weed the front yard flower beds. I took Mr. D outside with me to keep me company. About five minutes into my frantic weed pulling, Mr. D went into a barking frenzy. When I turned around to see what the ruckus was all about...I saw HIM, the animal that I named GEORGE...who was a huge curly horned Dall Ram (which is a male sheep). He was huge and as I looked on, he ducked his head in a full on frontal attack on Mr. D. Trying to protect me, Mr. D put himself between George and myself. The large beast hit D at freight train speed, slamming into Mr. D's head, knocking him out cold and then running over him. I screamed and chased the curly horned beast back a bit. With the Ram still pawing at the ground and readying himself for another charge, I quickly scooped up Mr. D and ran into the open garage and into the house. As I layed Mr. D onto my bed, I heard a loud crash inside the garage. I carefully opened the door to the garage to discover that George had attacked my motorcycle and knocked it over. But at least he was gone, the furry monster was no longer in sight. I quickly closed the garage door behind me and went to check on Mr. D's condition. By now he was slowly coming around, but very groggy. This was Mr. D's TBI! I did call the police to file a report. When the police came, the officer was very shocked at my story and looked at me at first with total unbelieve...as if I told him I had seen a UFO or some- thing. But soon they discovered that George was not a figment of my imagination and that he actually lived three streets over and belonged to some people who had multiple farm animals in their backyard. No charges were filed and I never saw George again. It wasn't long before those folks moved out of our neighborhood and I was very relieved to know that they were gone, and George was out of our life. I kind of understand why the police officer looked at me with such unbelief. I mean, who is truly gonna believe that I was attacked by a huge mountain sheep, while in town. It could only happen to me!

CHAPTER 9

THE DOLPHIN

Mr. D, who is our largest four-legged child, is totally obsessed with a dolphin shaped squeaky toy that we found at a local Walmart. My Lord, Mr. D played for hours every day with Dolphin, throwing it into the air and catching it and squeaking it to pieces. Unfortunately, poor Dolphin could only take so much abuse and fun before it began to fall apart, only held together by dog spit and air. Poor, poor Dolphin! Never again will he squeak.

Mr. D met us in the morning with this mangled corpse of a toy, and we felt horrible. We debated over coffee whether we should give the Dolphin a funeral or just throw it in the trash. That is when I got an idea to launch an international mission to find, if possible, the existence of another "Dolphin" of the same make and model. Little did I know, what a challenge I had taken on.

The Hunt Grew Long

Days turned to weeks, weeks to months. Deeper and deeper became Mr. D's depression. The problem was becoming more complex. This toy issue needed to be fixed soon. One day about two month into the "Dolphin" hunt, we went to a Ross store and I found on a clearance rack a very well built squeaky toy, shaped like a football: one that he couldn't pop and destroy in less than a second.

Much to my surprise, when we showed Mr. D, he was super exited and he has since become quite a wide receiver; he can catch that football like a pro!!! And he rarely if ever will miss a catch. While the football has been a great spirit lifter, it could never replace the joy that Mr. D experienced with Dolphin.

Then one morning while still trying to wake myself (even though I was on my second cup of coffee), I happened to check eBay again and then Amazon to continue the search. There it was! I couldn't believe my eyes! Dolphins, the same ones I had searched and searched for. Made in China and shipped from China. I didn't care, I would have drove to China if I could have. Quickly I ordered three as fast as I get my credit card out of my wallet, OMG, I celebrated for the day. Weeks later, we had "Dolphins" at my house.

CHAPTER 10

IN A PICKLE

The flaming heat of the relentless Texas sun beat down on my body, as I closely searched out the remaining vines of the scorched cucumbers that we planted in the spring. My husband canned "German Dills" and his famous "Bread & Butter" pickles, we loved them and gave them to friends and neighbors. This particular morning we had gotten up around 7 am and fed our zoo of loveable babies to include the birds and we had finished with our morning play that included tossing the football to Mr. D and getting the boy some well needed exercise. The other four smaller dogs are: Sam, our rescue Yorkie...who is very! Active; Weiner, who is a log of a dachshund, black and tan; Cinnie or Cinnamon is our Chihuahua and Sadie, a mini Schnauzer. OMG, what a crew of love, attitude and jealousy. You would think after being together for six years they would be angels...Ha, Ha! They are!!! But lets not push it.

So as I am searching for cucumbers I found a seven inch cuke that had escaped getting picked, so I picked it and layed it on the ground besides me and continued the search for more. Only finding a few more small ones, I had my hands full and I turned to go in...but, when I turned around... no big cucumber? Ok, I went in and put the others down and returned to the scene of the crime. Now what did I do with that pickle? Not on the ground, not on the fence. Not dropped back in the garden. "Man, I am really losing it." I said. Instead of telling my husband about this, I kept it to myself and decided...This was my caper! And I will get to the bottom of this pickle barrel, if it's the last thing I do! Inspector Pickle to the rescue! No really, where's the damn pickle? It didn't take long to deduce that the pickle in question, had not walked off by itself, so follow the yellow brick road...I went to Mr. D's room and there on his doggie bed next to his football was the green suspect cucumber with multiple tooth- mark impressions...the search was over...but, who or whom could have been slick enough to swipe it from under my nose? After what seemed like hours my deductive reasoning brought me to the knowledge that there was only one answer...There was more than one suspect...multiple perps! A professional job of at least a team of two. Then like a bolt from out the blue...I realized the only two dogs that could have pulled this off was Sam the Sneak...and The Big Kahoona...the "Boss" and King-pin... The infamous Mr. D. D being the brains of the job and Sam, his smooth operator in the field pulled this one off as smooth as glass. Goes to show ya if it looks like a football... it ain't always a football and it doesn't squeak! They both gave me this look... Vegetables...get 'em outta here!

www.ingramcontent.com/pod-product-compliance
Lightning Source LLC
Chambersburg PA
CBHW041132280526
45792CB00013B/2397